HOOVER SCHOOL
890 Brockhurst
Oakland, CA 94608

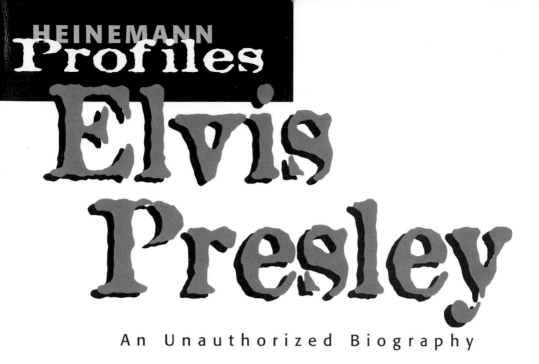

HEINEMANN Profiles

Elvis Presley

An Unauthorized Biography

Rupert Matthews

Heinemann Library
Chicago, Illinois

© 2001 Reed Educational & Professional Publishing
Published by Heinemann Library,
an imprint of Reed Educational & Professional Publishing,
Chicago, Illinois

Customer Service 888-454-2279

Visit our website at www.heinemannlibrary.com

Produced for Heinemann Library by Discovery Books Limited
Designed by Barry Dwyer
Originated by Dot Gradations
Printed and bound in Hong Kong/China

05 04 03 02
10 9 8 7 6 5 4 3 2

Library of Congress Cataloging-in-Publication Data
Matthews, Rupert.
    Elvis Presley / Rupert Matthews.
      p. cm. -- (Heinemann profiles)
    Includes bibliographical references and indexes.
    ISBN 1-58810-056-1 (library binding)
    1. Presley, Elvis, 1935-1977--Juvenile literature. 2. Rock musicians--United States--Biography--
Juvenile literature. [1. Presley, Elvis, 1935-1977. 2. Singers. 3. Rock
music.] I. Title. II. Series.

ML3930.P73 M38 2001
782.42166'092--dc21
[B]
                                  00-059747

Acknowledgments
The author and publishers are grateful to the following for permission to reproduce copyright material:Corbis, pp. 6, 7, 27, 30, 34, 46, 47, 48, 51; Peter Newark's American Pictures, p. 22; Popperfoto, pp. 20, 25, 35; Redferns, pp. 4, 5, 9, 10, 11, 13, 14, 17, 18, 29, 31, 32, 37, 39, 41, 42, 45; Topham Picture Point, pp. 28, 38.

Cover photograph reproduced with permission of E.T. Archive

This is an unauthorized biography. The subject has not sponsored or endorsed this book.

Some words are shown in bold, **like this.** You can find out what they mean by looking in the glossary.

CONTENTS

WHO WAS ELVIS PRESLEY?

Elvis Presley was called the "King of **Rock and Roll.**" His unique voice redefined popular music for a generation, and he set the pace for other performers who entered the world of pop music.

Elvis grew up in the poor area of a poor town, but his talent became obvious at a young age. He started out by singing at church services, revival meetings, and school concerts. Elvis then went on to perform at local halls and soared to national fame when he was still a teenager. Before long, Elvis's face was seen on record covers, television shows, films, key rings, watches, mugs, and playing cards. No singer before Elvis had achieved such enormous fame.

Elvis performs on his 1968 NBC television special.

After 1961, Elvis's singing career stalled as he concentrated on making several popular musical films. These films were hardly impressive, but Elvis's music was often great, and he made a lot of money. When Elvis returned to the stage in 1968, he proved that he was as dynamic as ever. However, overeating, too many sleepless nights, and abuse of **prescription drugs** wrecked Elvis's health. In 1977, at the age of just 42, Elvis Presley died.

But as a rock legend, Elvis lives on. His music continues to sell well, and his films are shown on TVs around the world. Some people refuse to believe that Elvis died so young and think he is hiding somewhere. Elvis built up a legend that has survived long after his death.

"When we were kids, all we ever wanted to be was Elvis Presley."
Paul McCartney, former member of the Beatles

A young Elvis Presley is shown on a postage stamp.

29 USA

ROCK & ROLL SINGER, 1935-1977

ELVIS

A Boy in Tupelo

Elvis Presley was born on January 8, 1935, in the small town of East Tupelo, Mississippi. His twin brother, Jesse Garon Presley, died at birth and was buried the next day. Elvis's parents, Vernon and Gladys, had married two years earlier. The family was poor but respectable. Elvis's childhood would be marked by a long struggle against poverty.

The house in which Elvis was born had been built by his father and some relatives in his grandfather's yard. The house measured just 30 feet by 10 feet (9 meters by 3 meters).

Elvis was born in this two-room house in East Tupelo, Mississippi, and lived there until he was thirteen.

Elvis at the age of three.

Vernon Presley had a stretch of low-paying jobs, while Gladys helped earn money by sewing or cleaning for wealthy local families. Despite their money troubles, the Presleys always found time for religion. It was at church where Elvis first showed his musical talents. By the age of three, Elvis had learned the more popular hymns and would sing along to them and dance up and down the aisles.

EARLY INFLUENCES

Elvis loved church music and was particularly drawn to African-American churches. However, because he was white, he was not always welcome and sometimes had to listen while sitting outside. At the time, racism divided black and white people in the United States, and sometimes members of the other group were not welcome. But Elvis was not discouraged, and he watched how the ministers and choirs used their bodies to keep time with the beat and emphasize the song's message.

In 1941, the United States entered **World War II.** The government's need for planes, tanks, guns, and other weapons meant better paid jobs, even in small towns like East Tupelo. For the first time in his life, Vernon had a steady job. He used the money to buy a second-hand car and a radio.

Segregation

Throughout most of the first half of the twentieth century, black and white Americans in the South were segregated. This meant that African-Americans and whites went to different churches, sat in different parts of buses, sat on different park benches, and used different drinking fountains. Segregationist policies were later recognized as illegal and were abolished after the Civil Rights Movement of the 1960s.

The radio introduced Elvis to **country music,** swing, and other new musical styles. He particularly loved the rhythm and blues performed by African-American musicians. With the family's extra income, Gladys had $10 to spend on Elvis's eleventh birthday present. She bought a guitar and persuaded Elvis's Uncle Luther to give the boy lessons.

To Memphis

In September 1948, Vernon was arrested for selling illegal whiskey. The local judge ordered him to leave Mississippi and never return. Elvis later recalled, "We left Tupelo overnight. Dad packed all our belongings in boxes and put them on the top and in the trunk of our Plymouth. Then we headed for Memphis." Memphis, Tennessee, was a large industrial city of 300,000 people. At first, Elvis found the city frightening.

Elvis aged about eight, with his father, Vernon Presley, and mother, Gladys

First Songs

I n Memphis, Vernon got a job in a factory and Gladys worked as a waitress. Together they earned just $35 a week and could afford only to rent a one-room apartment. In 1949, Elvis went to the L. C. Humes High School.

A teenage Elvis in costume. During his teen years, Elvis loved dressing in unusual clothes.

One girl at school recalled Elvis. "He was a very shy person, but he did carry this guitar with him." Elvis played the guitar in between classes to entertain his friends. One of these friends was Red West, a member of the football team, who shared Elvis's love of modern music. Elvis liked to visit Beale Street in Memphis, where he could listen to the African-American musicians who would later influence his own style of music so much.

A new look

In the autumn of 1950, Elvis got a part-time job at the Loew's State Theater selling tickets and popcorn and showing people to their seats. Most of the money went to help pay the family's bills, but Elvis spent some of it on stylish clothes. He liked pink shirts and black

Elvis, shown here with his parents in 1954, was just beginning to enjoy success.

pants. He also grew his hair long and slicked it back with hair oil. This cool new look didn't do Elvis any good at school, where he was picked on by other boys. One day, three boys cornered Elvis and threatened to cut his hair short, but Red West showed up and frightened the boys off.

In December 1952, a teacher talked Elvis into taking part in the school talent show. Elvis walked on, guitar in hand. "Then it happened," said Red West. "Elvis put one foot up on a chair to act as a prop, and he started to plunk away. When he finished, the kids went crazy. Elvis seemed to be amazed that for the first time in his life someone other than his family really liked him. As shy as he was, he had a definite magic on stage."

"Elvis stood out like a camel in the Arctic."
Fellow high school pupil

ELVIS THE TRUCK DRIVER

When Elvis left school in June 1953, his family was still short of money. So Elvis took a job as a truck driver for the Crown Electric Company. At the time, Elvis told a friend, "I don't need that much money, just enough for me and Mama to get by."

THE BIRTHDAY PRESENT

In August 1953, Elvis decided to make an inexpensive record of himself singing a song as a birthday present for his mother. He walked into the Sun Studios of the Memphis Recording Service, where he could record his voice for just $4. Marion Keisker, the studio assistant, thought Elvis had real singing talent, so she taped part of the recording.

Sun Studios was run by Sam Phillips, who also ran a small **record label** that sold songs by local bands to radio stations in the south. On June 26, 1954,

Elvis's style

"I sing all kinds. I don't sound like nobody." Elvis said in reply to Marion Keisker when she asked what style of music he sang. She was setting levels in the recording studio and needed to know if he would be crooning softly or playing loud. He misunderstood and thought she meant music style.

12

The Sun Studios in Memphis, Tennessee, where Elvis cut his first record and where he signed his first recording deal.

Phillips suddenly found himself without a singer. He asked Marion Keisker to call Elvis and ask him to come in for a trial recording. "I ran all the way," Elvis recalled. "I was there by the time they hung up the phone." Phillips later said, "Man, this was just Elvis on a guitar, and he could wail the heck out of a guitar. I heard him and that was it." Phillips got in touch with professional musicians he thought would work well with Elvis.

Sun Records

Sun Records had made records by well-known African-American blues musicians before, but southern white people had never bought such records. Phillips always hoped one day to find a white performer to introduce this kind of vibrant music to a white audience.

SUN RECORDS

At the urging of Sam Phillips, Elvis Presley teamed up with country guitarist Scotty Moore and bass player Bill Black to form a band called the Hillbilly Cats. On July 6, 1954, the trio went to Sun Studios to record a few songs. The first two songs were nothing special, but then Elvis began thumping out "That's All Right, Mama." Phillips was startled and ran excitedly through the studio. "What the devil are you boys doing?"

A recording session at Sun Studios with, from left to right, Elvis Presley, Bill Black, Scotty Moore and Sam Phillips

"Don't know," replied Elvis. "Well find out real quick," shouted Phillips, "and let's put it on tape!"

The song was recorded for release as a single and was in stores just twelve days later. Phillips took it to WHBQ, a Memphis radio station that had a rhythm and blues show called *Red, Hot, and Blue*. The DJ, Dewey Phillips, agreed to play the song. One schoolmate of Elvis recalled the evening clearly.

"My mom was all excited and called out to me to come in and listen to the radio as a boy from my school was singing. I knew it had to be Elvis. He was the only one whose singing was worth [anything]." "That's All Right, Mama" reached number three in the Memphis country charts in July 1954.

THE NEW STAR

As the record played for the first time, Dewey Phillips got so many calls from the public that he decided to bring Elvis into the studio. He called Sun Studios, and Sam Phillips raced to Elvis's home. But Elvis had gone to the movies! When Elvis finally got to the studio, he chatted nervously to the DJ, only to discover later that he had been live on air!

Elvis signed a recording contract with Sun Records, while Scotty Moore took charge of the live shows. Elvis wore an outrageous pink and white cowboy suit and, because he and Moore were from Memphis, they were billed as a **country music** act. But their thumping music and Elvis's wild dancing made them unlike any other country music act, and it drove the young audience wild. Elvis had managed to combine the feel and sounds of African-American music with the words and tunes of white music.

A SECOND OPINION

In September 1954, Moore booked a show for Elvis at Nashville's Grand Ole Opry, the biggest concert hall in Tennessee. It was to be the hall's first live radio broadcast. Unfortunately, the audience there was older than the young teens who appreciated Elvis, and the new band flopped. Jim Denny, the Opry's manager, told Elvis, "Listen boy, you should quit singing and go back to driving a truck."

Elvis decided he would give up music after playing one more gig, a radio show called the *Louisiana Hayride*. But the younger *Hayride* audience reacted enthusiastically to Elvis and the band was offered a regular contract. The next day, Elvis quit his job. Soon the band was playing almost every night at county fairs, bars, and clubs.

During this time, Elvis built up a huge fan base in the south. Audiences loved his good looks and flashy

Elvis the Pelvis

During his early appearances on stage, Elvis swung his hips in time to the music in a fashion no other singer had ever used. In **anatomy,** the pelvis is part of the hip, so newspapers started calling him "Elvis the Pelvis." At first, Elvis himself did not realize that it was partly his dance style that made him so popular. Talking about one appearance he said, "My manager told me that the audience was hollering because I was wiggling. And so I went out for an encore, and I wiggled a little more. And the more I did the wilder they went."

clothes. But the main attractions was his music and the extraordinary dance style that earned him the nickname "Elvis the Pelvis."

Elvis attracted young people as his main fans. Before World War II, many young people left school when they were twelve or fourteen to get jobs. Only the wealthy went on to college. However, during the 1950s, more young people stayed in school and worked part time. They had spending money without adult responsibilities. This group of people became known as "teenagers."

Elvis and Bill Black perform during one of their early tours.

> "You know if that young man keeps going like that, he's going to make it real big one of these days."
> Singer Slim Whitman, 1954

THE COLONEL

In May 1955, Elvis and the band joined the Hank Snow **Jamboree** tour. The tour brought Elvis to a new audience, and demand for his next single, "Mystery Train," boomed. The tour was also important in another way. Working for the Jamboree was **publicist** and manager **Colonel** Tom Parker. Parker saw Elvis as a major talent and decided to become his manager. The partnership lasted until Elvis's death.

COLONEL PARKER

Elvis signed a contract with his manager, Colonel Tom Parker, in August 1955.

Born Andreas Cornelis van Kuijk in the Netherlands, **Colonel** Tom Parker moved to the United States as a young man and spent some time in the army before joining a traveling carnival. He changed his name to make it easier to pronounce and became a full-time publicist and **promoter.** After meeting Elvis Presley during the 1955 **Jamboree** tour, Parker offered to handle all the business and promotional side of Elvis's career for 25 percent of everything Elvis made. Parker told Elvis, "You stay young and sexy and I'll make us both rich as **rajahs.**"

The Colonel put together a record deal that would make Elvis rich and famous. Ignoring offers from successful record companies Columbia-CBS and Atlantic, Parker went with RCA. The company put out records by performers the Colonel already managed, and Parker trusted them. The deal was finalized on November 20, 1955. Elvis took his money and rushed out to buy his mother a flashy pink Cadillac.

"When I met him, he had a million dollars worth of talent. Now he's got a million dollars."
Colonel Tom Parker

A FAST BUCK

Throughout the partnership, Elvis and Parker achieved amazing success, but they were often criticized by music executives for being more interested in money than in music. Often, Parker insisted that songwriters give Elvis a cut of their **royalties** before he would sing their songs, or he forced Elvis to perform on stage when he was sick. In truth, neither Parker nor Elvis really believed the fame and fortune would last very long. By the time they realized Elvis was an established star, they had become so accustomed to making money quickly that they could not break the habit.

"He can't last. I tell you flat. He can't last."
Jackie Gleason, TV producer, 1956

The first recording session at RCA produced one of Elvis's greatest hits, "Heartbreak Hotel." The song blended the raw energy Elvis used on the road with the skill and smoothness of professional RCA musicians and sound engineers. The single was released on January 27, 1956. By the end of March, it was number one on the **Billboard** Popular Music Chart and the **Country Music** Chart and number five on the Rhythm and Blues Chart. This told the nation that Elvis was a performer to watch.

NATIONAL TELEVISION

Meanwhile, Parker had booked Presley and the band to appear on television's nationally broadcast *Stage Show*, which was hosted by Tommy and Jimmy Dorsey. Elvis wore black pants and shirt with a white tie, specially designed to look good on black-and-white TV. The audience was packed with teenagers and when Elvis sang, they went wild. This guaranteed that Elvis would be invited back.

Next, Parker persuaded television's *Milton Berle Show* to part with $10,000 for a two-show deal. Elvis performed his gyrating dances that were so popular on stage, but they did not go over well with a middle-aged TV audience. Berle received more than 700,000 letters of complaint about the show.

Elvis and his band practice on stage for *The Ed Sullivan Show,* which was to take his musical style to a national audience.

On September 9, 1956 Elvis appeared on *The Ed Sullivan Show.* The show broke all records for **ratings.** Fifty-four million people, or about 82 percent of all American television viewers, tuned in to see Elvis rock through "Don't Be Cruel," "Hound Dog," and "Love Me Tender." A second appearance came in October, but it was the third show on January 6, 1957, that caused an uproar.

Sullivan had also received many complaints about Elvis' dancing, so he decided Elvis could be shown only from the waist up. This was designed to hide Presley's gyrations and to stop complaints, but Elvis refused to change his popular act just for the television cameras. Instead, he danced with renewed energy and the studio audience screamed and cheered louder than ever. Then Elvis decided to use his arms to make up for the fact his legs could not be seen. The performance was electrifying and seemed guaranteed to lead to new heights of controversy.

A REPUTATION IS SAVED

However, Ed Sullivan had begun to like Elvis during rehearsals. He put his own reputation at risk by announcing to his TV audience, "I wanted to say to Elvis Presley and the country that this is a real decent fine boy, and we've never had a pleasanter experience on our show with a big name than we've had with him." Elvis—who had never wanted or deserved a bad reputation—was thrilled. Colonel Parker was thrilled, too.

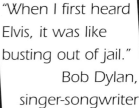

"When I first heard Elvis, it was like busting out of jail."

Bob Dylan, singer-songwriter

To Hollywood

The first Elvis movie, *Love Me Tender,* was originally conceived as a dramatic western. The movie was hurriedly rewritten as a musical when Elvis was cast.

In the spring of 1956, **movie producer** Hal Wallis of Paramount Pictures saw Elvis perform on *Stage Show.* Wowed by the show, Wallis called **Colonel** Parker and arranged for Elvis to fly to Hollywood for a screen test. Elvis read a few lines of script. Wallis must have been impressed, because Paramount Pictures immediately offered Elvis a three-movie deal worth $450,000.

Elvis's first movie, a dramatic western starring established Hollywood stars Richard Egan and Debra Paget, was at first called *The Reno Brothers.* But the film was renamed *Love Me Tender* after the song Elvis sang in the movie. Unlike some temperamental stars of the day, Elvis was always on time and knew his lines.

When the movie opened in New York on November 15, 1956, a huge crowd of teenagers showed up. The police had to block the road and clear a path for the stars and press photographers. In less than a week the film turned a profit—nobody in Hollywood could remember a movie having such immediate box-office success before. Paramount immediately recognized a money-maker and put Elvis into the starring role of *Loving You*. In this film, Elvis played a character like himself, a poor boy who makes a fortune as a singer. Elvis sang eight songs in this movie. One of the songs, "Teddy Bear," was released as a single and hit number one on the pop charts.

GRACELAND

In February 1957, Elvis had a bad scare. He was getting out of his car at home when a group of teenage fans leapt at him and tore his clothes off as souvenirs. Vernon Presley rushed out and pulled Elvis away. The Presleys decided they had to move to a house with a wall around it. The money from the movie contracts gave them the cash to buy a large mansion in Memphis called "Graceland," set on fifteen acres (six hectares). The family totally redecorated the house, equipping it with air conditioning and a racquetball court. The main entrance was torn down and replaced with a gate that was to become famous. The famous Music Gate, as it was called, had iron gates featuring musical notes and a guitar-playing Elvis. Worried that fans who pushed against the gates might be hurt, Elvis insisted that there be no sharp edges on the metalwork.

Meanwhile, Elvis called on Red West to act as a bodyguard. Soon Marty Lacker joined Elvis to make sure transportation was always available and that Elvis arrived on time. Sonny West, Red's brother, and Lamar Fike were hired to help out with security and luggage. Together, these four old school friends formed a vital support group for Elvis and were soon known as the "Memphis Mafia."

THE GOLDEN BOY

Elvis's next movie was *Jailhouse Rock*. He received 50 percent of studio profits as well as his fee of $250,000. Elvis was allowed to arrange the songs and dance routines himself, and he took full advantage of the opportunity. The most spectacular sequence in the movie is the dance routine to the title song. The stark black and white images of jail bars and a line of dancing "convicts" is one of the most memorable images of 1950s rock music. But the added responsibility had its down side. Elvis had to show up for work at 7:30 a.m., and he rarely left

Suit of gold

One of Presley's most famous 1950s outfits was a dinner suit made of gold lamé. But he did not like it very much and often wore only the jacket. Eventually, **Colonel** Parker borrowed it and wore it more often than Elvis himself.

the set before 6 p.m.
By the end of
shooting, Elvis was
exhausted.

Meanwhile, Elvis's
live shows grew
bigger and more
profitable as the
months passed. In the
recording studio,
Elvis went back to
his musical roots
with a number of
gospel songs.

Then he made "The
Elvis Christmas
Album," a collection
of songs that ranged

Jailhouse Rock, from **rock and roll** tracks to seasonal children's
which was shot songs and religious hymns.
in 1957,
featured Elvis Elvis's next movie revealed his talent as an actor. In
singing thirteen *King Creole,* Elvis plays a somber, violent character
songs. who works in the seedy nightclubs of New Orleans.
Elvis acted well, and the film received good
reviews. This was also partly due to the direction of
Michael Curtiz and performances by **Oscar** nominee
co–stars Walter Matthau and Carolyn Jones.

G.I. Blue

When Elvis was at the height of his fame, fate dealt him a serious blow. At the age of 23, Elvis was called up before the **draft** board to serve in the army. **Colonel** Parker worked out a deal with the army. Under the deal, Elvis was allowed a 60-day delay to finish his movie and recording work. He was finally inducted into the army on March 24, 1958.

The military and the media

Most people expected Elvis to try to avoid the draft or to take it easy by performing for the troops. However, Elvis was determined not to demand special privileges. He was given the **dog tag** number 53310761 before being sent off for six months of basic training at Fort Hood, Texas. The press was allowed to film every detail of Elvis's first day. Cutting his famous long hair to the regulation **crew cut** caused a press sensation. When it became obvious that Elvis had behaved patriotically, putting his career on hold to serve his country, many of his critics were won over. Elvis had lost his "bad boy" image.

The draft

During the 1950s in America and many other countries, young men could be "drafted"—or called up—for military service. They could put off being drafted by going to college. If they were married with children, they could avoid the draft altogether.

"It's tough living up to an image."
Elvis Presley

Colonel Parker did not want two years in the army to hurt Elvis's career, so he persuaded Elvis to spend his **leaves** recording rock and roll songs. With the old Sun Studios songs, Parker had enough music to keep adoring Elvis fans happy for many months. Only time would tell if they would stay loyal to a star they could no longer see on stage or in the movies. When Elvis was asked if he would continue recording songs during his time in the army, he replied, "I'm in the army. That's my job now."

Elvis's army uniform was a far cry from his original pink and black get-up. Aside from a few carefully managed press photo sessions, Elvis stayed out of the limelight when he was in the army.

GRIEVING

In August 1958 Elvis's mother died. Elvis was devastated, and for the rest of his life he found it difficult to talk about her. After twenty days of leave, Elvis was sent to Germany to join the U.S. troops stationed there. When the ship docked at Bremerhaven on October 1, 1958, it was met by a large crowd. As soon as Elvis appeared, the crowd surged forward with such force the military police had trouble holding it back.

"He was an extremely pleasant, sincere young man who took the time and trouble to speak to everyone he met."
Major Ed Miller, U.S. military base commander

Forbidden movie

○ The final scene of the movie *Loving You* shows Elvis singing
○ to a packed theater, with his parents sitting in the back row.
○ After the death of his mother, Elvis refused to watch the
○ movie ever again.

PROMOTION

Elvis was given the task of maintaining and driving a **jeep.** His love of cars made this as much a hobby as a job. He was frequently sent around Germany driving officers or delivering packages and messages. A surprise inspection of the Fourth Armored Division showed that Presley's was one of the few vehicles to achieve top grades for care and maintenance. Elvis soon became a corporal, and later, a sergeant.

PRISCILLA BEAULIEU

Elvis found an old friend at his base in Germany. Captain Keisker was the father of Marion Keisker, the Sun Studios receptionist. Keisker introduced Elvis to Captain Joseph Beaulieu, who had a step-daughter named Priscilla. Elvis and Priscilla soon became close. Because the girl was only fourteen, Captain Beaulieu was strict about when and how often the two could meet.

Meanwhile, Parker and Elvis began planning to relaunch

A teenage Priscilla Beaulieu writes a letter to Elvis after his return to the states. The two dated in Germany for several weeks.

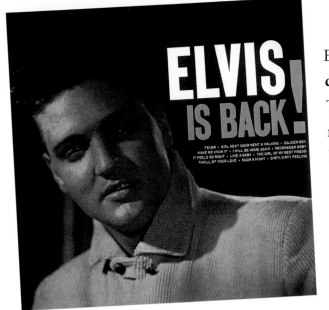

The album cover for "Elvis Is Back!" announced what the world had been waiting for.

Elvis's career after his **discharge** in March 1960. They decided to release a movie called **G.I.** *Blues* based on Elvis's time in the army. To speed up production, scenes without Elvis were shot before he left the army. Parker made sure that songs for a new album were written and arranged and that a recording studio was available after his discharge.

On March 1, Elvis left Germany. Priscilla came to the airport to wave him goodbye. Newspaper reporters were shocked because it was the first time anyone outside the army knew of the romance. Priscilla soon became known as "the girl Elvis left behind," but neither she nor Elvis spoke publicly about their romance. As Elvis made his way back to the United States during his discharge, the army was happy to go along with the various interviews arranged by **Colonel** Parker. After all, army officials were eager to show that being **drafted** was not the nightmare some young men thought it might be.

"Elvis died when he went into the army."

John Lennon, former member of the Beatles

THE FILM YEARS

E lvis returned to Graceland, a retreat that was largely his own creation. The living room had a a grand piano and dark blue curtains edged in gold. The dining room had a pure white carpet, and the dining room table and chairs stood on a large black marble central panel. The music room was decorated in red. In the basement was the famous Jungle Room, which featured Hawaiian footstools and thrones covered in fur and decorated with wooden carvings of ancient gods. Elvis covered the floor and ceiling in this room in thick, dark-green carpet. On one wall, water flowed down a stone sculpture with plants growing out of it.

Graceland, the home Elvis bought in March 1957, was where he lived for the rest of his life.

The sumptuously decorated dining room at Graceland, like all the rooms in the mansion, was designed by Elvis himself.

BACK TO WORK

As soon as Elvis was back at Graceland, Parker took him to Nashville to record new songs. It was immediately clear that Elvis still had his magic. In fact, critics said he had grown more dynamic and mature in style. Elvis also flew to Florida to record a television show called *Welcome Home Elvis*. The **G.I.** *Blues* movie was released in October and was a hit. This encouraged Paramount to get another Elvis movie under way as quickly as possible.

THE WRONG CHOICE

The movie *Flaming Star* was released in December. It was different than the films Elvis fans were used to seeing. There were only two songs. Elvis played a mixed-race Indian living with his white father's family in the Old West. Although Elvis gave his best movie performance yet, the film was a flop.

FORMULA FOR SUCCESS

Colonel Parker and Elvis learned a lesson from this failure. In the next film, *Blue Hawaii,* Elvis sang fourteen songs in a beautiful location, again playing a poor musician who eventually makes good. Elvis fans flocked to see their hero, and the exotic locations and popular co-stars guaranteed a good-looking and successful film. Although the movie lacked the raw power of *Jailhouse Rock,* it was amazingly successful at the box-office. It is, perhaps, the classic Elvis movie. Encouraged by its success, Parker and the Hollywood bosses decided to use the same formula in the future. For his efforts, Elvis would be paid $1 million per movie, plus a share of the profits.

Elvis and his co-stars pose in a publicity shot for the movie Blue Hawaii. The film became the most successful Elvis movie.

Since returning from Germany, Elvis had dated several girls, but none of the relationships had lasted long. At Christmas 1960, he invited Priscilla for a visit. Aware of Presley's many short-lived relationships, Captain Beaulieu allowed the visit only after Elvis agreed to a **chaperone.** In May 1962, Priscilla turned eighteen. Because she was now considered an adult, her step-father allowed Priscilla to come and live at Graceland while she finished school.

In 1966, Elvis recorded the album "How Great Thou Art," which won him his first **Grammy** award. But Elvis was focusing most of his efforts on movies, sometimes completing three in a year. Meanwhile, big changes were taking place in the world of pop music. The Beatles, the Rolling Stones, and other groups were experimenting with new forms of music. Elvis, who still put out music he made popular during the 1950s, was becoming out-of-date. Recognizing the real danger facing his career, Elvis decided to take a new direction.

THE COMEBACK

The decision by Elvis to relaunch his music career may have been inspired by his personal life. In May 1967, Elvis married Priscilla in a private ceremony at the Aladdin Hotel in Las Vegas. Elvis was dressed in a dark brocade **tuxedo.** Priscilla had her hair in the bouffant style fashionable at the time, dyed black to match Elvis's. It was a surprisingly simple event with only a handful of family guests. There was, however, a showy six-layer cake decorated with red roses and sugar hearts. The cake was specially made for the reporters covering the event.

This extravagant wedding cake was baked for Elvis and Priscilla, who married in Las Vegas on May 1, 1967.

NEW BEGINNINGS

Priscilla gave birth to their daughter, Lisa Marie, in Memphis the following February. Elvis became a devoted father, making time in his busy schedule for their new child. His happiness and enthusiasm for life spurred him on to look for new projects.

The previous September, Elvis had gone to the RCA Studios in Nashville for a major recording session. He wanted to try out ideas and arrangements. Elvis hadn't performed live for years, and was nervous about going on stage again. In the end Elvis decided that he would make his comeback on a recorded television show with a live audience, scheduled for Christmas 1968 on NBC. The format would give producers time to edit out any mistakes before the show was broadcast.

"As the years went by I missed audience contact," Elvis said. "I was really getting bugged. I couldn't do what I could do, y'know. They (film directors) would say "action" and I would go "uh-uh.""

At a photo shoot on February 5, 1968, the press and public got their first view of the newborn baby, Lisa Marie.

The '68 special

The show's producer, Steve Binder, saw it as a way to relaunch the energy and power of Elvis's 1950s stage shows. The idea was that several big-set numbers would begin and end the show, with a center spot when Elvis and his band would appear on a small stage before a live audience. **Colonel** Parker thought the live spot was too risky and wanted Elvis to simply sing a few songs and a Christmas hymn or two. Elvis went along with Binder's suggestion.

But the center spot and the live audience had Elvis deeply worried. When Elvis tried out some of the stage movements from the early days, he found himself out of breath. This caused him to begin a strict diet and exercise routine to get fit. But without a live audience, it was difficult to predict how successful the act would be. Elvis was visibly shaking when he finally strode out on to the stage. However, the show turned out to be a triumph. Scotty Moore, who hadn't performed with Elvis for some time, was very impressed. "In the '68 special he was just as much like he was in the first years, '54 or '55, as you could ask him to be," Moore said later.

"He gave everything that he had—more than anyone knew he had."
Critic Greil Marcus, on the 1968 TV show

After weeks of editing, cutting, and re-recording of some songs, the finished special was ready for broadcast on December 3, 1968. It was the session with a live audience that relaunched Elvis's career. Dressed in a black leather jump suit, Elvis began the show dancing alone. Then the band came on stage and sat on stools with him. Elvis chatted to the audience, bringing them in on the act. They loved it, and the fans at home were thrilled to see a new, more dynamic Elvis.

Elvis performs on stage during the live spot of his 1968 Television Special. Many critics thought it was the best part of the show.

The special re-established Elvis as a popular major rock star. But Elvis wanted one more chance at acting, and he chose to star in a western called *Charro*. Elvis fans were surprised that there was no music in the movie and that Elvis grew a beard for the part. *Charro* did not do well, and Elvis gave up any idea of being a serious actor.

THE VEGAS YEARS

During the late
1960s, Las Vegas
began to draw
big-name
performers to its
casinos and clubs.
By the time Elvis
arrived in 1969,
Las Vegas was
known for its
lavish stage
shows as much as
for the gambling
to be found
there.

After his great success with TV and records, Elvis wanted to go back to where he started—touring with a live show. **Colonel** Parker decided that in order to cope with the huge number of fans, Elvis should play stadiums large enough to hold thousands of people. Parker was looking for suitable places when the International Hotel in Las Vegas offered Elvis $1 million for a four-week appearance.

SHOWTIME

In July 1969, Elvis flew to Las Vegas to start rehearsals with the band. By July 31, he was back on stage. The act opened with a dark stage, suddenly lit by a single spotlight. Elvis stepped into the light

As the years passed, Elvis took to wearing fancy white suits with turned-up collars and flared pants. They became the standard costume adopted by many Elvis imitators.

just as the band burst into song. No longer wearing casual clothes, Elvis wore a jet black suit with flared sleeves and high collar, an outfit that gradually developed over the coming months into the glittering jumpsuits that became an Elvis trademark. Elvis also began to practice some moves that became famous in later shows. He would kneel down at the front of the stage to talk to or touch the first few rows of fans. Toward the end of the act, he would ask for a handkerchief, use it to wipe his face, and hand it back to the swooning fan.

The shows were booked solid, and the hotel asked Elvis to stay for two more weeks and then return again the following year. When Elvis returned for 60 days in 1970, the number of tourists visiting Las Vegas skyrocketed. The city council estimated that profits from gambling, drinks, and food rose by ten percent when Elvis was in town.

ON THE ROAD

After Las Vegas, Elvis started a grueling tour of American cities, beginning with the Houston **Astrodome** in Texas. These enormously profitable shows finally convinced Parker that Elvis could make as much money touring as he did in the movies. Parker extended the tour and persuaded Elvis to spend nearly all his time on the road. Over the next seven years, Elvis visited 125 cities and played more than a thousand concerts, an average of three per week. Every one of the concerts sold out.

SUCCESS WORLDWIDE

Although Elvis had decided not to make any more musical movies, he could not ignore the film business entirely. In December 1970, he starred in *Elvis—That's the Way It Is*, a documentary about Elvis on tour. It was a huge success with people who were not able to see his concerts.

The hit records continued to pour out. But perhaps the greatest achievement of Elvis's comeback happened in 1973 when *Elvis: Aloha from Hawaii*, a televised concert held to raise funds for cancer research, was broadcast from the Hawaiian islands. Audiences in Japan, South Korea, Australia, New Zealand, Vietnam, Thailand, and the Philippines were able to see the show live. Time differences meant that people in the United States had to see the show the next day.

THE END

Elvis, Priscilla, and Lisa sit for one of their last family photos. Despite the divorce, Elvis remained devoted to his daughter.

Even though Elvis was enjoying success again during the early 1970s, his personal life was in trouble. The constant touring was a strain, and Elvis did not see Priscilla as often as he would have liked. In October 1973, after six years of marriage, they divorced. Lisa Marie was only five then, but her parents remained friends. Priscilla became a frequent visitor to Graceland or to wherever Elvis happened to be on tour.

In 1976, RCA pressured Elvis to record some entirely new songs. The concerts were still selling out, but they focused on old favorites and did not help sell records. Elvis came up with excuses to avoid the task, only agreeing after RCA said he could record the songs at Graceland. The session produced a group of songs that ranged from from outstanding to mediocre, but the album sold well.

Health problems

Unknown to his fans, Elvis was becoming seriously ill. Early in 1974, Elvis failed to appear on a television gospel show due to "ill health." On several occasions he slipped into Baptist Hospital in Memphis to be treated for exhaustion, eye strain, or **pneumonia.** But the most dangerous health problems were caused by his diet. From childhood, Elvis had loved southern country cooking, which includes **grits, corn pone,** biscuits, and deep-fried sandwiches— food designed for hard-working farmers, not singers who spent days sitting around. Elvis would pile on weight, then go on a crash diet before going on stage.

What was far worse was his increasing reliance on **prescription drugs.** Although the drugs were legal, Elvis took them in reckless quantities. He took sleeping pills and **stimulants** to cope with stress on the road, then appetite suppressants and laxatives to cope with eating binges after a stage tour. The drugs were originally prescribed by Elvis's own doctor, who had been treating him since 1966. At first, the doctor encouraged Elvis to exercise regularly and reduce the fat in his diet. But the doctor eventually gave up the struggle and he, along with various other doctors, began giving him prescriptions for large quantities of drugs.

The Final Months

By the summer of 1976, Elvis was clearly sick, although the cause of his illness was not public knowledge. One critic wrote, "Elvis strode on stage puffy-faced and dressed in a gaudy costume with a six-inch belt, he posed for thousands of instamatic flashcubes during a quick run through of "CC Rider." He still has a remarkably strong, deeply resonant voice that, unfortunately, he displayed only rarely. He spent most of his time tossing scarves like **Mardi Gras** favors to the audience, shaking hands, receiving flowers and presents, and kissing the women persistent enough to break through the throng to the stage and pull themselves up close enough to the King that he didn't have to lean over too far."

In March 1977, Elvis was forced to cut short a tour and was rushed to a hospital. He was able to resume the tour the next month, but by then he was clearly very ill. On the night of August 15, 1977, Elvis couldn't sleep. He sat down at his piano to play some old favorites. Sometime after dawn, he stopped playing and picked up a religious book. A few hours later, he was found slumped on the bathroom floor. He was

"I wouldn't have cared if they had to wheel him out in a wheelbarrow— it was still Elvis."

Scott Rohde (fan talking about a late 1976 concert)

Elvis performs in a dramatic suit first seen in 1975. By this date his health was suffering and he sometimes appeared puffy and out of breath on stage.

rushed to Baptist Hospital, but was pronounced dead at 3:30 P.M. The immediate cause of death was listed as heart failure. However, the cause of the failure was not stated on the death certificate and has been the subject of debate ever since.

THE LEGEND LIVES ON

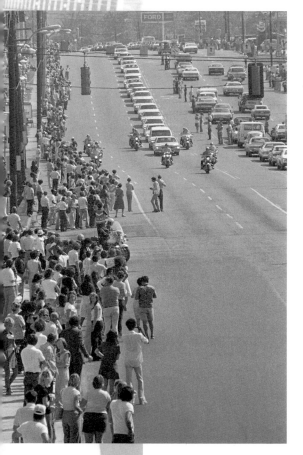

The news that Elvis was dead spread quickly. By 6:30 P.M., a crowd of more than 20,000 people had gathered outside Graceland. They stood silently in shock. A reporter recalled hearing the news. "I was visiting the *Chicago Sun-Times* . . .when a guy ran by yelling, 'Elvis is dead!' Seconds later a voice boomed across the newsroom, 'Stop the presses!' It was a moment I'd only seen in the movies. To this day, I still get chills when I think of that editor ordering the *Sun-Times*'s presses to stop."

A PRESIDENT PAYS TRIBUTE

The funeral was held a few days later at Forest Hills Cemetery in Memphis, where Gladys Presley was buried. More than 200,000 people showed up to line the route. U.S. President Jimmy Carter said, "Elvis Presley's death deprives our country of a part of itself. He was a symbol to the people of the world of the vitality, rebelliousness, and good humor of this country."

Elvis is buried in a private burial plot at Graceland.

Elvis was dead, but his adoring fans would not let his legend die, too. So many people visited the grave that the bodies of both Elvis and his mother had to be transferred to a private plot at Graceland. Around the world, fans set up **posthumous** fan clubs and began creating their own memorials to the King.

REMEMBERING ELVIS

Elvis left most of his possessions and the rights to his work to his daughter, Lisa Marie, with Priscilla as trustee until Lisa Marie turned 25. Priscilla Presley decided to devote her life to safeguarding the memory of Elvis and ensuring that her daughter had a secure inheritance. She said, "I don't want Lisa, when she's 25, to say 'Where's my Dad's stuff?'"

Priscilla created Elvis Presley Enterprises and invested money left by Elvis to open Graceland to the public. The house and grounds were restored to the way they were when Elvis was at the peak of his career. Elvis's will declared that any family members who wanted to live at Graceland could do so, and some still do.

Today, Graceland is the second most visited tourist attraction in the United States, with more than 600,000 visitors each year. Only the White House is more popular. On display at Graceland are the original 1955 pink Cadillac that Elvis bought his mother, along with a Cadillac with a customized gold-plated dashboard that he drove the day before he died.

THE LEGEND

Even in the new millennium, the Elvis legend lives on. When Elvis died in 1977, there were 38 Elvis impersonators who earned money singing his songs at private parties or charity events. Today, there are an estimated 11,000. Paramount has released many of its popular Elvis movies on home video. Even toy manufacturers got in on the act. There was even a special Elvis Barbie doll. His records continue to sell in vast numbers. More than one billion have been sold worldwide. This makes Elvis the top-selling artist of all time. Elvis earned more than 100 platinum or gold

Elvis Presley impersonators take part in an Elvis Contest in Bangkok.

records. Meanwhile, the second most popular band, the Beatles, had just 45.

More amazing than the continued success of Elvis records and **memorabilia** is the persistent legend that Elvis did not really die. Some people think that Elvis instead retreated from the pressures of stardom to retire to a quiet hideaway somewhere.

Soon after Elvis's death, one witness reported, "I saw Elvis in at the local diner down here in Overbrook. He was drinking a Diet Coke and eating some fried chicken. When he left, he thanked the cook for a mighty good meal and said he sure was thankful. He paid with a hundred dollar bill and told her to keep the change. He then got in a 1953 Chevy Bel-Air custom turquoise-and-white auto. It had tinted windows and he said to the driver 'Let's go, Bubba,' and he was gone." Similar claims have been reported more recently. No doubt they will continue to be posted on the Internet as long as the Elvis legend lives on.

THE CHANGING VIEW OF ELVIS

John Lennon said, "Before Elvis there was nothing." Elvis said that he was lucky to come into the music industry at the right time, when teenagers were ready to experience a new trend. Both points of view underestimate the phenomenon of Elvis's music. He produced a new and unique style that influenced musicians worldwide. In fact, Lennon also said, "If there hadn't been an Elvis, there wouldn't have been the Beatles."

Early on in Presley's career, many influential people in the United States disliked him. Before he booked him for his famous three shows, Ed Sullivan had said, "I won't touch Elvis with a long stick." Frank Sinatra, a star popular with a previous generation of music fans, said Presley's music was deplorable. Other people called it "vulgar" and "talentless."

"Elvis Presley is a weapon of the American psychological war aimed at infecting a part of the population with a new outlook of inhumanity."
Youth World, East German communist newspaper

Religious leaders said that Elvis was not the kind of boy they would like their children to see. After Elvis's military service, and the repackaging of the singer into a clean-cut, all-American boy, Elvis was eventually praised by Sinatra. In fact, Sinatra later sang

along with Elvis on the *Frank Sinatra Show*. Gone was the rebel with the long hair and outrageous clothes, and gone, too, was the Elvis who was described as "so different in everything he did."

After the 1968 Christmas special, critics saw a real possibility of the old Elvis returning—"finding his way back home," as one critic put it. But the concert schedule that followed wrecked his marriage and, eventually, his health. A stronger person

Elvis Presley performs with Frank Sinatra in 1960.

might have handled fame better, but Presley's childhood poverty probably made it hard for him to quit making money. No doubt, Elvis relied on the adoration of his audience as much as he relied on the drugs he used to get himself through the day.

Presley's death was an international tragedy, but Elvis the rock legend lives on. Bruce Springsteen, a rock legend in his own right, said this about Elvis: "There have been several contenders, but only one King."

FILMS AND RECORDS

MOVIES

1956	*Love Me Tender* (Twentieth Century Fox)
1957	*Loving You* (Paramount)
	Jailhouse Rock (Metro-Goldwyn-Mayer)
1958	*King Creole* (Paramount)
1960	***G.I.*** *Blues* (Paramount)
	Flaming Star (Paramount)
1961	*Wild in the Country* (Paramount)
	Blue Hawaii (Paramount)
1962	*Follow that Dream* (Paramount)
	Kid Galahad (Paramount)
	Girls! Girls! Girls! (Paramount)
1963	*Fun in Acapulco* (Paramount)
	It Happened at the World's Fair (Metro-Goldwyn-Mayer)
1964	*Kissin' Cousins* (Paramount)
	Viva Las Vegas (Paramount)
	Roustabout (Paramount)
1965	*Girl Happy* (Paramount)
	Tickle Me (Paramount)
	Harum Scarum (Paramount)
1966	*Paradise, Hawaiian Style* (Paramount)
	Spinout (Metro-Goldwyn-Mayer)
	Frankie and Johnny (United Artists)
1967	*Double Trouble* (Metro-Goldwyn-Mayer)
	Clambake (United Artists)
	Easy Come, Easy Go (Paramount)
1968	*Stay Away Joe* (Metro-Goldwyn-Mayer)
	Speedway (Metro-Goldwyn-Mayer)
	Live a Little, Love a Little (Metro-Goldwyn-Mayer)
1969	*Charro* (National General Pictures)
	The Trouble with Girls (Metro-Goldwyn-Mayer)
	Change of Habit (Metro-Goldwyn-Mayer)
1970	*Elvis—That's the Way It Is* (Metro-Goldwyn-Mayer)
1972	*Elvis on Tour* (Metro-Goldwyn-Mayer)

Singles—Million-Copy Sellers

All RCA Recordings

1956
"Heartbreak Hotel"
"I Was the One"
"I Want You, I Need You, I Love You"
"Hound Dog"
"Don't Be Cruel"
"Blue Suede Shoes"
"Love Me Tender"
"Any Way You Want Me"

1957
"All Shook Up"
"That's When Your Heartbreak Begins"
"Teddy Bear"
"Loving You"
"Jailhouse Rock"
"Treat Me Nice"

1958
"Don't"
"I Beg of You"
"One Night"
"Wear My Ring Around Your Neck"
"Hard-Headed Woman"
"I Got Stung"

1959
"A Fool Such as I"
"A Big Hunk o' Love"

1960
"Stuck on You"
"It's Now or Never"
"A Mess of Blues"
"Are You Lonesome Tonight?"
"I Gotta Know"

1961
"Surrender"
"I Feel So Bad"

"Little Sister"
"Can't Help Falling in Love"
"Rock-a-Hula Baby"

1962
"She's Not You"
"Return to Sender"
"Where Do You Come From?"

1963
"One Broken Heart for Sale"
"Devil in Disguise"
"Bossa Nova Baby"

1964
"Kissin' Cousins"
"Viva Las Vegas"
"Ain't that Loving You Baby"
"Wooden Heart"

1965
"Crying in the Chapel"
"I'm Yours"

1968
"If I Can Dream"

1969
"In the Ghetto"
"Suspicious Minds"
"Don't Cry Daddy"

1970
"The Wonder of You"

1971
"Kentucky Rain"

1972
"Burning Love"

GLOSSARY

Billboard Magazine
magazine that covers the music industry and publishes lists of best-selling records in the United States

chaperone person who accompanies young, unmarried girls on a date

colonel high military rank, but also a title given as an honor

corn pone corn bread made without milk or eggs that has been deep fried

crew cut very short hair cut achieved by running electric clippers all over the head

discharge process of leaving the army, navy, or other branch of the military

dog tag metal identity tag worn by members of the armed forces

draft compulsory, or mandatory, military service

G.I. soldier in the U.S. Army; short for *government issue*

gospel style of religious music that features simple melodies and harmonies

Grammy award given to singers and songwriters by music industry specialists

grits coarsely ground grain eaten as a type of hot cereal

jamboree word often used to describe a loud stage show

Jeep word derived from *GP*, or general purpose; nickname of a rugged, off-road vehicle used in the army

leave short break in service from the military

Mardi Gras celebration that occurs in late winter before the Christian season of Lent

memorabilia items associated with a specific person or time, such as old newspaper articles, photos, or concert programs

Oscar award given to an outstanding actor, director, or specialist in a movie

pneumonia serious disease of the lungs

prescription drugs medicines that are legal but available only if prescribed by a doctor

profit amount of money left over after the expenses of running a business have been paid

posthumous after death

promoter person who organizes and finds funding for a concert or a sports event

publicist person who organizes publicity, such as advertisements, posters, and newspaper stories, on behalf of another person

rajah type of prince in India famous for great wealth and a luxurious lifestyle

ratings estimate of how many people watch a particular television show

record label company that produces music on records, tapes, or CDs for sale

review article in a newspaper or magazine giving an expert opinion of a record, concert, movie, play, or book

rock and roll style of music developed during the 1950s that features drums, guitars, and a strong beat

royalties payments made to performers whenever their work is sold or performed

stimulant drug that speeds up the actions of the body for a short period of time

World War II war fought between 1939 and 1945 between Germany, Japan and their allies, and the United States, Britain, Russia and their allies

MORE BOOKS TO READ

Gentry, Tony. *Elvis Presley.* New York: Chelsea House, 1994.

Harding, Melissa. *Elvis Presley* New York: Chelsea House, 1997.

INDEX